RESTART

HOW TO GENERATE AN EXTRA 10-80 CAR
DEALS IN THE NEXT 30 DAYS FROM REFERRALS

Gus T. Skarlis

LTV Press
Las Vegas, NV

Copyright © 2015 by Gus T. Skarlis

All rights reserved. No part of this publication may be reproduced, distributed or transmitted in any form or by any means, including photocopying, recording, or other electronic or mechanical methods, without the prior written permission of the publisher, except in the case of brief quotations embodied in critical reviews and certain other noncommercial uses permitted by copyright law. For permission requests, write to the publisher, addressed "Attention: Permissions Coordinator," at the address below.

Gus Skarlis & LTV Press
ReferralDriven.com
Ordering Information:

Quantity sales. Special discounts are available on quantity purchases by corporations, associations, and others. For details, contact the "Special Sales Department" at the address above.

Book Title/ Author Name. —1st ed.

ISBN-13: 978-1514308677
ISBN-10: 1514308673

CONTENTS

Chapter 1: My Back Story 1

Chapter 2: On The Right Track 4

Chapter 3: College Dropout 6

Chapter 4: Getting My Chance 8

Chapter 5: The Software Revolution 10

Chapter 6: Referral Marketing Education 12

Chapter 7: The Big Blowout 13

Chapter 8: The AutoNation Days 15

Chapter 9: The Doug Spedding Days 17

Chapter 10: The Sonic Chance 20

Chapter 11: Taking Chances 22

Chapter 12: The Shark Tanks 26

Chapter 13: Back In The Car Business 28

Chapter 14: The Start Of A Referral Revolution 32

Chapter 15: Why Referral Marketing Now? 34

Chapter 16: Your Current Obstacles 37

Chapter 17: Take Action 42

Chapter 18: Identify Your Best Targets 46

Chapter 19: Leverage Your Network 52

Chapter 20: Contact These Businesses 56

Chapter 21: Build Your Audience 64

Chapter 22: You're Not Making It Easy 67

Chapter 23: Solutions 72

Chapter 24: Getting More Referrals Has Nothing To Do
           With Your Reputation 77

Chapter 25: New Client Kit 79

Chapter 26: Answer These Questions 81

Chapter 27: Build Value 86

Chapter 28: Make It Impossible For Your Competitors 89

Chapter 29: How Much To Pay For A Referral? 93

Chapter 30: Lifetime Client Value 95

Chapter 31: How To Pay Your Referral Fees 97

Chapter 32: Hire A Referral Manager 101

Chapter 33: You're Not Thinking Big Enough 104

Chapter 34: 21 Advanced Referral Strategies 105

Chapter 35: Action Steps 116

Dedicated to all those people who believed in me.

"Legacy is more valuable than currency."

"If you educate your current clients you will have a "mobile sales force" helping you spread the message about your business...."

"When the recommendation is coming from a family or friend it's not considered an advertisement."

"Referrals are not given but earned."

"Why is Facebook the most used platform on the planet? Because a friend told a friend told a friend."

"Lifetime Value is the only number that matters."

"You need to be connecting with LOCAL businesses if you want referrals."

—**Gus T. Skarlis**

Quick Note: You might be located in a state that does not allow "Bird Dogs" or referral payments.

Don't worry because the strategies you are going to learn about in "RESTART" can be substituted with points, discounts and even be used for lead generation.

The principles are the same whether you are paying a fee or not.

Thank you for reading and I look forward to meeting you soon.

CHAPTER 1

My Back Story

I was born on August 20, 1974, in Mason City, Iowa; a small town of approximately 30,000 people, located halfway in between Minneapolis and Des Moines.

Before I was born, my father, who was an auto mechanic by trade, was offered the local Datsun (Nissan) franchise by the retiring owner.

He took over the dealership in 1969 then in 1986, bought the local Honda and Oldsmobile franchises from the retiring owner.

Growing up in the car business was really fun.

My dad was always driving new vehicles, and I got to go down to the dealership on Saturdays and help plug the holes after the mechanics had sprayed the rustproofing.

It was my first job.

I was paid $1.00 a day—$0.25 of which was spent on donuts during our 10 am "shop break."

When I was seven, I joined the swim team. I trained hard and eventually went on to become a two-time state champion and state record holder in high school.

On my 14th birthday, I was given the gift of a "real job."

My parents took me down to their friend's restaurant, where I was hired as a busboy.

My job started immediately. Just my luck: the dishwasher called in sick that day, so I spent my first week doing dishes for $4.75 an hour.

Over the years I would eventually move up to server, bartender, catering and events.

I loved the restaurant business. It was fast paced, action packed and full of characters. At 14 I was learning a lot.

Because my town was so small there wasn't a whole lot going on in the summers so when school let out I would take on more jobs.

I used to watch a local doctor's mansion and take care of his six dogs while he was at his lake house.

Looking back it was the best job I ever had. I got paid to feed and walk the dogs around his compound and got to play with all of his toys.

He had a go cart track that circled the property.

Another neighborhood doctor owned an acreage where I would mow and keep up on all of the landscaping.

I also worked as a lifeguard at the local country club and taught and private swimming lessons.

As you can tell, I was really busy. And it paid off: I was making about $500 a week and boy did I love having all that money in my pocket.

When I went back to High School in the fall I was the only kid in high school that didn't have a lunch ticket; I paid cash every day for my lunch.

I even got my first bank loan during this time.

There was this Onkyo stereo system with Polk Audio speakers from Sound World that I just had to have.

Because I was working so many jobs and had income, my dad co-signed my loan which was $58.55 per month for 3 years.

I paid off the loan in 8 months!

CHAPTER 2

On The Right Track

My high schools days were filled with fun and a lot of activities.

I played the saxaphone in both symphonic and jazz band, was on the swim team and worked 30 hours a week at the restaurant.

My sophomore year I was a state champion and then my junior year I repeated and our team also won the title.

During senior year of high school I was recruited by a few colleges to swim for them.

My top picks were… University of Miami, Auburn and a few others but the only one I wanted to attend was Babson College in Wellesley, MA.

I was accepted to Babson College which was U.S. News & World Report's #1 Business College in 1992.

However, since we were in a recession and the car business was not that good - my dad could not afford to pay the $20,000 tuition fee.

Back then student loans were not as easy to get as they are today so I went 90 miles down the road to University of Northern Iowa and swam for them.

This was a big disappointment for me and still haunts me today.

It's probably my single most motivating factor because all I wanted was the opportunity to go to Babson and I couldn't.

I think in some sort of strange way I'm still trying to prove that even though I did not attend Babson I'm still as good as those who did.

One of my long term goals is to start a scholarship at Babson College that would allow student athletes like myself to have the opportunity to go to Babson.

During the second year of college at UNI I blew out my shoulder and had to give up swimming for good.

CHAPTER 3

College Dropout

Without a job to keep me busy and bored with school, I dropped out of college and went back home and told my parents I wanted to sell cars.

Needless to say they were not happy with my decision but what else was I going to do?

A few days later I showed up at the dealership ready to start selling some cars.

When my dad got in I asked him what he wanted me to do.

He said, "First off, you need to learn about the cars you are going to be selling."

So I grabbed a few brochures and started reading them. He took them away from me and said, "Follow me."

We walked back to the shop and he said, "The only way you're going to learn about these vehicles is to clean them."

> **For the next 18 months my job duties included: detailing vehicles, running the lube rack, parts delivery, floor cleaner, painter and car parker.**

At the time, I didn't think it was such a great idea, but looking back, I'm glad he made me do it.

The most important thing I learned was that if you don't take care of them in service they won't come back and buy a vehicle later.

It also taught me enough about the vehicles to enable me to speak authoritatively about our products.

After a year and a half of working "in the back" I asked him if I could start selling cars.

His reply was, "We don't have enough business to add another salesperson to the floor, so until it picks up, just stay in the back."

Naturally, I was disappointed.

I bugged him every week and eventually suggested that I wouldn't take any clients on the floor; I'd just call the orphan owners.

CHAPTER 4

Getting My Chance

After constant nagging to him about my "no risk" offer he finally agreed, so I grabbed some old deal files, a phone and started calling clients.

That first month, I sold three cars... all to my friends. The next month, I sold nine.

During those few months of cold calling, I read every book about sales that I could get my hands on.

This was before Amazon, so I would either have to go the library or try to find books for sale in trade magazines.

All that reading must have helped because...

When business picked up the following spring and my dad let me on the floor where I could take ups, I was off to the races!

In just a few months, I was selling more than 20 cars a month!

One of my secret strategies was this...

At the time, my friend Doug who was a busboy and server with me at the restaurant now owned it and every Friday & Saturday night, I would be his "host."

It was my job to greet all of the guests as the front door and ask how many were in their party and seat them at their tables.

Since I'd spent so much time in the restaurant business growing up, it was like second nature to me.

I worked for free.

The real reason I did it was that every weekend I got to shake hands with between **two and three hundred potential clients.**

Working at the restaurant meant I could start conversations with people I would never otherwise have met and develop relationships with his loyal clients.

I made a lot of friends at the restaurant and even more sales from "helping out" on the weekends.

Because I did this almost everyone in town knew that I sold cars and it only cost me a few hours of my time… time well spent.

CHAPTER 5

The Software Revolution

One day I went to a seminar at our local community college, NIACC, and the guest speaker was Harvey McKay.

If you don't know who Harvey McKay is I would highly recommend you go out and buy his books.

Harvey had just developed a new client tracking and mangement system called Sharkware.

Today they are called CRM's.

> **I was so excited about Sharkware I bought the software on the spot.**

But the best part is - I didn't even have a computer!

Remember, this was in the early 90's.

So, I went down to First Interstate Bank and asked if I could get a loan for a computer.

Because I had a great credit score they gave me a loan and I walked across the street to the IBM store and bought my first computer.

After I got Sharkware installed I started adding all of my clients information. I added birthdays, key codes, VIN numbers, paint codes, trade in information and notes about each client.

Having all of this data at my fingertips allowed me to crank up my marketing.

I started sending out a monthly newsletter, birthday cards and oil change reminders.

It got to the point where I was sending out so much mail I would have to wait until my dad left for the day before running the envelopes through the Pitney-Bowes machine.

He would have had a heart attact if he knew how much I was spending on postage.

But it was working. I was now selling 25+ vehicles each and every month.

CHAPTER 6

Referral Marketing Education

By this time I had a few hundred clients in Sharkware and I was really finding my stride.

I was selling cars, building my brand and looking for ways to expand our dealerships' sales.

So my next move was to set up my referral marketing program.

Trying to find any information about what was working in the auto industry was really tough.

No one seemed to be talking about referral marketing so I called my my Uncle George who had a great referral marketing plan in his business.

We'll get into more details about how his referral program would change history later in the book.

Fast-forward about six years to mid January of 2000.

CHAPTER 7

The Big Blowout

My dad and I got into a very heated argument about how to run the dealership, where to spend the advertising budget and how many vehicles we should have in inventory.

You know: the general family issues everyone has!

I was so upset I walked 2 miles home in -10 degree weather.

I finally found the courage to stand my ground and gave him an ultimatum where I wrote all my demands and expectations down and had my mom give it to him.

Either he gives up some control or I was leaving. He had 3 days to decide.

During those 3 days I stayed home figuring out both plan A and plan B.

Plan A was where I mapped out the next 10 years of our dealerships' future.

Plan B was where I called up the general manager of Las Vegas Honda, Kalei Dudoit who I had met a few times at the National Honda Dealer convention and asked him if they were hiring.

I guess stubbornness runs in the family, because he refused the ultimatum.

> **So the very next day I flew out of Minneapolis with $1500 cash in my pocket and landed in warm, sunny Las Vegas looking for an opportunity.**

I arrived at McCarren, went to the phone banks, selected the lowest price hotel on the Strip which happened to be a Travel Lodge and called them.

They picked me up and I checked in.

Not knowing where the dealership was at I asked the front desk clerk how to get there.

She told me it would be cheaper to take the bus so a few hours later I hopped on the bus, went to the dealership and asked for a job.

CHAPTER 8

The AutoNation Days

The very next day, I was selling cars. I went from running a car dealership to starting on the front lines again, but I was happy, and that was all that mattered.

For the first 18 months, I worked every day. I didn't have a car, and without wheels, I really couldn't go anywhere.

I lived on East St. Louis Ave., a few blocks from the dealership, which meant it was just a short walk to work everyday.

After a year, I was promoted to Internet Director.

> **Soon, our internet department was firing on all cylinders and we consistently ranked in the top 10 of all 380 AutoNation dealership.**

One day out of the blue, I got a call from AutoNation corporate.

They wanted to know how I was selling so many cars. My response was simple: I was nice to people!

Then AutoNation showed their hand: what they really wanted from me was a step-by-step description of my process. So I wrote a process manual.

Thinking other dealers would also want this information, I had a bunch of these manuals printed up.

In addition, I had a website built so I could sell this "secret" information to other dealers, too.

Now, you have to remember this took place in 2003, when most dealers were swearing off the Internet.

Needless to say, it didn't sell too well.

In fact, the same manual I wrote back in 2003 sells better *today* than when it was written 11 years ago—and the funny thing is that I haven't changed a thing!

You can find it on Amazon it's called... **"How To Build The Most Successful Automobile Internet Department EVER!"**

CHAPTER 9

The Doug Spedding Days

A few years later, I got a call from Doug Spedding who was a car legend.

He needed some help setting up his Internet Department at his Nissan store and he was told I was the best in the country at the time.

Doug Spedding has trained and mentored some of the best auto guys.

Kalei Dudoit who was my GM and now VP for AutoNation was trained by Doug.

So was Don Forman who is one of the top Nissan dealers in the country as well as at least more 10 dealer-owners that I personally know of.

Working for him was an opportunity that I felt would help further my career.

> **Leaving Honda and Kalei was actually harder than leaving my dad because it was the first time that someone actually believed in me and gave me a chance to prove myself.**

Plus, the team we had at Honda was so great.

It was the best store I ever had the opportunity to work for and am very grateful for the people I met and the friends I made.

In fact, we are all still great friends. 15 years later.

I got to the Nissan store and it was a mess. A complete disaster.

So with some hard work, hiring new people and getting processes in place we turned the store around.

Within 24 months we went from selling 150 vehicles to over 480 vehicles.

It was a wild and crazy ride. Hours were long. Paychecks were huge. It was crazy!

Doug Spedding and John Kelly, the GM, also gave me the opportunity to showcase my skills.

I got to work in finance where I was the top producer for 24 months straight.

I was also the New Car Director overseeing 8 million in new vehicle inventory.

Mr Spedding always wanted the inventory done by hand so I had to handwrite everything. NNA.net was useless to me because he wouldn't accept a computer report.

They also let me run a team and build their internet department from scratch.

It was fast and furious but the hours and demands were getting to be too much.

I had met a girl and wanted to spend more time with her.

CHAPTER 10

The Sonic Chance

Having quite the reputation in the Las Vegas market I would get calls from other dealers trying to hire me away. I rejected all of them for years.

Then one day I got a call from Pat Hickey who was looking for an internet director at his Sonic Store.

I said no because I was very happy where I was working at but he persisted and then he threw down all his cards.

> **He finally told me his GSM was Brad Lea.**

Brad was a legend in Vegas.

He developed the Real Deal Lease presentation and was probably the best car guy in Vegas at the time.

Thinking that it might be a good move for my career to keep learning from the best I finally said YES.

It was a great move.

Brad is one of those guys I instantly felt a connection with.

He was a hustler and he was very motivating. We sold a lot of cars and had a lot of fun.

At the time he was also selling his online video training platform called **LightSpeedVT.com** to dealers which was his way to get out of the long hours working in a dealership requires.

After a while and seeing what guys like Brad and others were doing I decided to venture out on my own.

CHAPTER 11

Taking Chances

In 2007, left the car business and started a marketing company that sold marketing and mailing lists.

It was called BusinessList.com, and it took off like gangbusters.

Before long, I started using my profits to develop other sites, businesses and ideas.

During the next few years I worked for Brad on the side at LightSpeedVT.

I can vividly remember Brad talking to Grant Cardone on the phone trying to get Grant to put his training on the LightSpeedVT platform.

Grant kept on saying "No" but Brad called almost every day and never gave up.

Now Brad's company is one of the biggest—if not the biggest—Online Virtual Training companies in the world...

I learned many life lessons from Brad.

A year later, I developed an application that allowed car dealerships to sell extended warranties online.

You can't believe the number of extended warranties that are sold by third parties.

These clients buy vehicles on eBay, Craigslist and AutoTrader, as well as through classified ads—but they'll never walk into to your dealership to buy a warranty.

> **It failed miserably… to this day I don't know why.**

I still have the platform because one thing I've learned is that I'm usually way ahead of the curve.

In 2009, I started MobileWebsites.com; a software application that could create a mobile optimized site in 30 seconds and wrote a few books about mobile development.

The reason I bring this up is because when you have so many great ideas, you absolutely need to execute them.

After a few years of running MobileWebsites.com I sold it.

CHAPTER 12

The Shark Tanks

Since I was functioning in large markets with billion-dollar potential, I learned that the fastest way to build a business was by raising money and connecting with the players in the space.

In order to see if I could raise funds, I put out profiles on Angel.co and a number of other venture capital sites.

I really didn't want to raise money because I wanted to grow my business organically but I wanted to find out what I could learn from the big players.

I took a total of 17 meetings with venture capitalists in locations such as Silicon Valley, Los Angeles and even Austin, TX.

> **Every single one went well. The investors all loved my ideas and application.**

I recorded the meetings and took copious notes so I could parse everything down afterwards.

The one common theme I noticed was this:

Venture capitalists all use leverage, whether that's a client list, a brand or even intellectual property.

And the number one question every VC firm asked me was this:

> **"What are you doing right now to leverage your existing client base to grow revenues?"**

Just think about it: all 17 firms I met with asked me that exact same question.

And that made me realize that venture capitalists know something about sales that most business people don't.

And that is… Your #1 asset is your client database.

At the time, I decided not to accept any funding.

Looking back, I probably should have but at that moment in time, it wasn't the right choice for me.

So I continued to build my businesses organically.

CHAPTER 13

Back In The Car Business

Fast-forward to 2012.

One morning, I got a call from a guy I used to work with asking if I could fill a finance position for a few weeks until he could find a suitable replacement.

This Ford dealer was a Time Magazine's Dealer of the Year award winner so I figured, **"What the heck, let's see if I'm really as good as I thought I was."**

During my years out of the car business I wrote a book about my time as a finance manager.

I'd been out of the car business for seven years but excited about changing gears.

As I got into the swing of things I found that some things were exactly the same, but there were also many changes, including a lot more paperwork.

I had to learn the lender programs and get back in the groove of getting paper bought because the director was more of a figurehead than a working director.

> **Once thing that really bothered me was that every day, we had to email Excel files to the 4 desk managers, GSM and GM with notes about why our deals were still open.**

To me, this felt like a complete waste of time because every manager still came back to the finance department every 15 minutes asking why a deal was still open.

I got tired of telling them to go check their email.

Being the idea guy that I am, I figured I could improve our process.

I designed a simple website where we could type in each client's name, sales person, finance and insurance person, desk manager and some notes about why the deal was open.

The best part is that they could see the open deals report from any computer or mobile device.

It's called OpenCarDeals.com and if you haven't seen it you need to check it out.

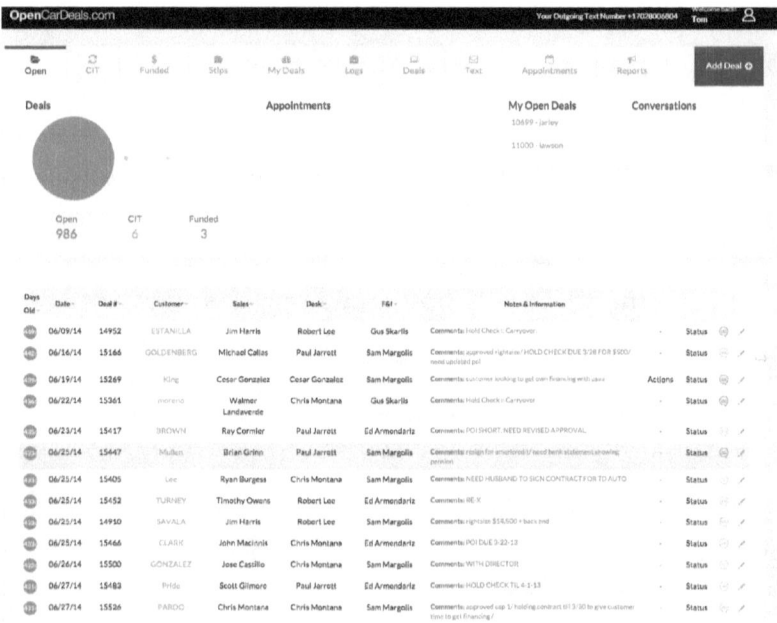

The entire team started to use OpenCarDeals.com and everyone loved it.

We kept coming up with new ways to make it better.

Before long, I had a team of three developers working full time on all of the features we wanted to implement.

I had spent over $50,000 to build and develop OpenCarDeals.com.

After using it for about 12 months and spending all of my own money I asked the GSM if he could give me $300 per month to cover the costs of the servers and bandwidth.

At the end of the month, our finance director notified me that we were no longer going to be using OpenCarDeals anymore.

I was shocked. I was pissed.

There was no reason given. I could not understand why they would not support me and my efforts to help make things better.

During my time at this store I was the top finance producer and helped take the finance department numbers from $1200 PVR to just short of $1900.

I wrote it off to typical car dealer politics and stayed for another 4 months, then left.

The one lesson I've learned in life is that if people are not going to support you then get rid of them.

So that's what I did.

CHAPTER 14

The Start Of A Referral Revolution

You're probably wondering, "What does all of this have to do with referrals?"

Well, a lot, actually. Over the years, I've kept thinking about what those venture capitalists asked me:

"What are you doing right now to leverage your existing client base to grow revenues?"

You see, when I learned that venture capitalists all know traditional marketing and advertising don't work anymore, I also learned one secret that's rarely talked about.

> **That secret marketing strategy is called Referral Marketing.**

Before venture capitalists invest in any company, they use a formula that accurately determines whether that company will be successful.

This formula is based on referral marketing.

Here's how it works in the simplest terms:

If a company can acquire a client at a break-even profit, and that client has the potential to send between one and three new clients to the business, then the company will be successful...

It's that simple.

> **After 20 years in the car business, software business and development space I decided to dedicate the next 40 years to building the best referral marketing platform for auto dealers.**

Referral marketing is not new... just new to you -- and what I'm going to share with you in these pages will completely change the way you look at referrals.

Let's get started...

CHAPTER 15

Why Referral Marketing Now?

Auto sales are back on track. The banks are loaning money. Rebates and incentives are good.

You are busy and this is exactly why you need to "restart" your referral program right now.

> **The goal of any referral program is for every client you have to generate 3 additional sales from THEIR friends and family.**

It's simple math. The more vehicles you sell the more clients you have and connections you make.

Look at every vehicle you sell as losing 3 future car deals… because that is exactly what's happening.

A referral program with a defined process will allow you to capture that business you're currently missing.

> **A referral program allows you to focus on the long term growth of your dealership.**

When developed and built the right way a referral program will allow you to generate additional sales, easy sales, profitable sales.

Think in these terms for a second.

If you sell 150 vehicles per month that's 1800 new clients per year.

1800 people bought from you because they like and trust you.

Those 1800 know at least 1 person that will be buying a vehicle in the next 12 months.

That's a minimum of 1800 opportunities you're missing right now.

Referral marketing is about your audience.

The bigger your audience the more opportunities you will have and this is why right now is great time to get it "restarted."

Whichever way you look at it, a referral program is a great asset.

It's going to generate more sales, more profit per transaction, more revenue and a referral program will increase the value of your dealership.

> **A great referral program and plan is going to build your business much quicker than your competitors.**

You're going to put the other dealerships in a position where they'll have to spend more money per car deal.

So while you might be spending $200, $300 or $400 a deal, they're going to have spend somewhere between $600 to $800, maybe even $1000 a deal.

Why?

Because it's just that much harder trying to compete against a dealership that was referred!

They can spend as much money as they like on newspaper, TV and online advertising, but it's nothing compared to the trust you gain if your clients' friends say, "Hey, you need to see Joey down at ABC Motors."

That person's going to see Joey at ABC Motors—no matter what the competition's advertisement says.

When a dealership has a great referral program in place every person you sell should lead to 3 additional sales and grow your dealership exponentially.

This is why you need to "restart" your referral program TODAY!

CHAPTER 16

Your Current Obstacles

After working with over 100 dealers it became apparent that that the reason referral programs weren't working in most stores was simply lack of education.

I can say with a high probability that no one has ever sat down with you and showed you how to develop a referral program at your dealership.

There are "experts" with products and solutions for everything else but nothing **dedicated** for referral marketing for auto dealers.

Go take a look in Automotive News, Ward's, and any other trade publication you will not find anyone talking about growing your dealership with referrals.

It's a shame because if you go outside of the auto industry you'll find great examples of companies that went from nothing to billions of dollars --- and it all was accomplished through referral marketing.

Paypal. Dropbox. Facebook.

You've been taught all your career. Generate more leads. Sell more vehicles.

This business plan will work until it doesn't, but if you really want to expand your sales and grow your dealership long-term you need to integrate referral marketing into your mix.

I know many of you have tried some form of referral marketing and failed.

It's OK. You are not alone because other dealerships are facing the same exact problems that you are with referral marketing too.

Your Staff.

If you are like most dealerships you "train" your sales staff to ask for referrals when they've made a sale.

That's not going to work. And the reason it's not going to work is because...

- Salespeople are scared to ask YOUR clients for referrals.

- Salespeople feel awkward talking about referrals.

- They don't feel like it's okay to ask for referrals.

- **Most of your staff are trying to "get out" of the car business.**

One common theme that I've seen over the years is that…

Your staff will only ask for referrals when they remember to and when they feel like it… no matter how much you "train" them or talk about it.

This is unacceptable.

It's your business, your risk and your money at stake...

It's your duty to have a referral process in place.

> **You can not let your sales staff dictate when and how they are going to ask for referrals.**

There must be a process and plan otherwise you're just wasting everyone's time.

This book is going to show you exactly how to set up your referral program so you can sell more vehicles, for more profit and build a long-term business.

Quit talking about your referral program.

The reason you're not getting very many referrals right now is because you're talking about it.

What you need to be doing is getting people signed up for your referral program.

> **Your #1 goal is to get as many people signed up for your referral program as possible.**

If I had to guess...

You have a page on your website with a form where clients can send you a referral.

You probably also have something printed on your business cards mentioning your referral program and maybe even an email template that you send out through your CRM.

In your mind you think you have 3 channels where clients can send you referrals.

But in reality you have ZERO.

You know why Target, Kohls, Albertson's and just about every large retailer has a reward program or discount club of some sort.

So YOU'LL sign up.

> **It's an old psychology trick called a "Micro-Commitment".**

When you sign up for something it's YOU that has made the conscious decision to take action.

It's you who said…

"Sure I'll give you my email address or phone number and carry this card in my wallet or keychain in exchange for extra deals or discounts."

And this makes all the difference in the world.

It's the same reason why you have your clients initial or sign the worksheet before you take it up to the sales desk.

If they'll sign once, they'll keep on signing.

You need to get your clients to sign up for your referral program and use this micro-commitment to your advantage.

By getting people signed up they are telling you…

"Yes, it's ok if you send me marketing messages."

I'll talk about the marketing messages and communication channels you'll be using in the next few chapters.

Are you starting to see the psychological differences between what you're currently doing and what you could be doing?

> **You can easily get people signed up for your referral program by using a few of the resources you already have at your dealership.**

CHAPTER 17

Take Action

The first step to getting people signed up for your referral program is to build a web page with details about your referral program.

A video explaining how your program works with some information is best, but make sure you buy a separate domain for your referral program sign ups.

This way you can send any marketing message, campaign or person to your referral sign up domain.

If you send people to your main website to sign up they will get lost and you'll lose the opportunity to get them signed up.

After you get your referral sign up domain and page set up the next step is to get as many "eyeballs" as possible to view your referral page.

Here's a secret strategy only a few people in the world know how to do...

Action Plan: Put a referral program sign up landing page on your WIFI network.

I'm guessing you have free Wi-Fi at your dealership, so service clients waiting for their vehicles can use your Wi-Fi to browse the Internet, right?

Let me tell you how this all came about…

I was at Lifetime Fitness, trying to log into their Wi-Fi.

However, before I could gain access to the Internet, I was shown the following offer: If I referred a friend and that friend joined the gym, I'd receive "LT Bucks."

I wanted to know how Lifetime Fitness managed to send people to this page before gaining access to the Internet, so I contacted a few people in the wireless world.

I learned that the gym had put a landing page on their router because they actually had more visitors on their Wi-Fi network than on their website.

Go look at your website's statistics, you'll probably see that you have more visitors on your WIFI network than your website too.

So here's how you can put a landing page on your WIFI network and get more people signed up for your referral program.

After a client selects your Wi-Fi network—but before he can get onto the Internet—you're going to show him a landing page with an option to join your referral program.

If he selects, "Yes," he'll be taken to your mobile optimized sign-up page where he can register.

This is another reason why you need to have a separate domain for your referral signups.

Do you think that will encourage a few of your service visitors to sign up?

Just one sign-up a day equals more than 350 new referral signups per year.

You'd have to estimate that this alone would have to be good for between 20 and 30 extra car deals per year, right?

Putting a landing page on your WIFI network gives you the ability to promote your referral program to this untapped traffic sources.

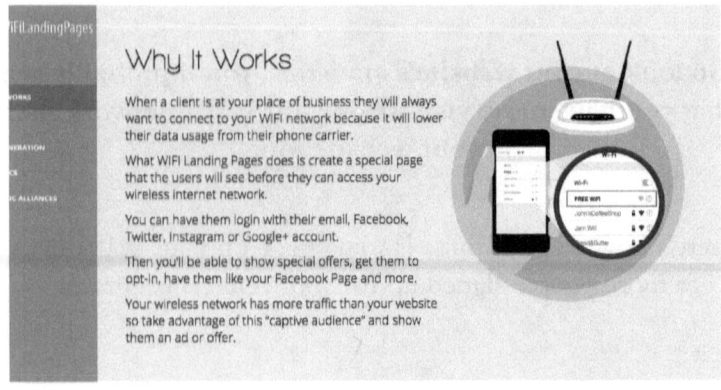

> **I loved this strategy so much I started a company called WIFILandingPages.com**

Action Plan: Promote Your Referral Program Everywhere.

The faster you get people signed up for your referral program, the sooner you'll start receiving referrals.

Every time you have contact with a person, you should be promoting your referral program.

No matter whether you're at the grocery store, gas station or golf course, everywhere you go, you and your staff should be asking people…

"Are you signed up for our referral program?"

If they aren't, give them your referral website, and encourage them to sign up.

Print messages on your RO's, invoices, business cards, flyers and mention it in your ads.

Anywhere you can promote your referral message the better.

> **The more people you have in your referral network, the more vehicles you'll sell.**

CHAPTER 18

Identify Your Best Targets

Remember your goal is to get as many people signed up for your referral program as fast as possible.

This way when that vehicle conversation comes up your client can talk about your dealership and send the referral prospect information to you.

Here's the four groups of people you'll need to focus on getting signed up.

1. Just-sold clients
2. Clients in your DMS
3. Leads in your CRM
4. Referral partners

The first group are you're "just-sold clients."

These are probably the easiest people to get signed up, but you have to ask them at the right time.

Most dealers have their salespeople ask for referrals during the delivery of the vehicle— which is the absolute worst time!

Put yourself in your client's shoes for a few seconds.

He's been at your dealership for a few hours.

He's tired, he's hungry, but most importantly, he's super excited about his new vehicle.

All he wants to do is go home and show it to his friends.

He definitely doesn't want to start writing down names and phone numbers of possible referrals.

Never ask for referrals this way.

If you want to increase your referral signups at the time of sale, the absolute best way to do this is to have your finance managers introduce your referral program in their office.

There are a few reasons for this.

First, with most of us using e-contracts nowadays, there's less time for your finance manager to find common ground.

When your finance manager is going over the soft forms, he can lead in with...

> *"Most of our business comes from referrals. Hopefully you feel good about doing business with us and would consider recommending your family and friends to us."*

Now, most clients will say, "Yes, of course! You guys have been great!"

Then your finance manager can go on to explain how your referral program works, how simple it is and how much your client can earn.

When your finance manager is talking about your referral program, you want him to mention the referral fee amount at least a few times.

That way, your client will know how much money he'll receive when he sends you a client.

Let me give you an example of why it's important.

When the objection of, "I can't afford it" comes up, your finance manager can simply respond with:

> *"Remember, our referral program pays you $200 for every client you send us. That will cover $17 of the $32 difference to protect your vehicle. Now, I'm sure you have a lot of friends, family and co-workers who'll all be buying a vehicle in the next year. So all you have to do is let them know how great you were treated here—and the extra coverage to protect your vehicle is costing you next to nothing! Just one referral a year; that's it. You can do that, right?"*

You can adjust the pitch accordingly, but you get the general idea: by introducing your referral program in your finance office, you'll not only get your clients signed up, you'll also sell them more products.

Next up is Group 2 and we're going to use a tool you already have in your dealership: Your CRM.

And we're going to use it to get a lot of people signed up for your referral program in just a matter of weeks.

How many leads do you have in your CRM?

If you have to guess, you'd probably say between 2,000 and 50,000, right?

But the question you need to be asking yourself is,

> **How many of these leads are signed up for your referral program?**

It does not matter if they bought a vehicle from you or not… every lead in your CRM should be should be sent an invitation to join your referral program.

The fastest way to introduce your CRM leads to your referral program is through email so get a campaign started and get these prospects signed up.

Just imagine, if only 2 percent of your CRM database actually sent you a referral, how many extra car deals is that?

The 3rd group is the holy grail of referral prospecting because it has your sold clients.

It's your DMS.

How many clients do you have in this database?

100,000 or more?

With this group you should take the time to set up a direct mail, email and telemarketing campaign to get everyone in this database signed up for your referral program.

Now, it's important to understand that it doesn't stop at your clients.

> **You also need to get your vendors and suppliers signed up, because they're all potential referral partners.**

They know you sell cars; but they don't know about your referral program.

What you need to do is get them signed up, because since they do business with you, they'll feel obligated to send business your way.

Once you have a business signed up then send an email to the HR person or owner of each vendor asking them to get every employee signed up for your referral program.

Before you start any marketing campaigns from your DMS system or CRM application, I advise exporting both of these lists and then de-duping them against each other to make sure that you're not sending multiple messages to the same clients.

All you have to do is tell your database developer to use address and phone number as the primary keys.

By doing this, you'll make sure you only have one unique record for each client.

RESOURCE:

> **If you need any help de-duping your DRM and CRM lists, you can email me at gus@referraldriven.com and I'll get our database adminstrators to do it for you.**

Are you starting to see the long term vision and why it's important to get as many people signed up for your referral program?

CHAPTER 19

Leverage Your Network

Now we are going to change gears and really explode your referrals opportunities by making business connections.

> **Without looking at your records, I want you to list the top five business in your area that have sent you a referral over the past 12 months.**

Can you list any of them?

How many business owners in your town do you actually know and talk to on a regular basis?

It's crucial to understand that if you want your dealership to be included in automotive conversations, you need to connect with local businesses in your area.

> **If you really want to have an ultra-successful referral program, you need to get as many business leaders and owners signed up as possible.**

But before discussing how you're going to do that, we need to go back and learn from my uncle George.

What my Uncle George did to get even more referrals for his home improvement business was to make friends with all of the painters, landscapers, construction teams, pool builders, restoration businesses, carpet cleaners, snow removal companies and architects in his community.

Why?

Because these types of professionals were always having conversations about home improvement.

In fact, oftentimes they were actually at a prospect's house when the subject of home improvement came up.

So what would happen is that a painter would be on a job, and the homeowner would ask him if he could recommend somebody to install new gutters or siding.

And guess whose name always came up? Uncle George.

> **To get this same strategy to work for your dealership, all you have to do is start contacting local businesses and invite them to join your referral program.**

Here's another example:

I've been in 17 meetings with venture capitalist firms for some of my other projects and I noticed that all of their deals were done with a single phone call.

Have you ever watched Shark Tank?

Let's say you want to get your sports drink sold in stadiums across the country.

- Mark Cuban can make one phone call and get it handled.
- You want your new gadget on QVC? Lori Grenier can make it happen with an email.
- Want to license your product to China? Mr. Wonderful just has to send a text message.

Why is it so easy?

Because these people all have networks they know they can trust and count on.

Get it?

> **It's all about who you know and who knows you… right now, no one knows who you are.**

Sure, they've seen your ads and have driven by your dealership.

But they don't know you, and that's why you aren't getting referrals.

Your dealership isn't being talked about by the decision makers in your community.

It's a very simple solution…

Start connecting with local business owners, and become the dealer they can trust and count on.

The only way this is going to happen is by you going out and meeting people.

However, there's a very specific strategy you need to follow:

1. Find a referral partner where people are having conversations about vehicles. The most logical starting point would be to look at local insurance agents, tow truck drivers and small, independent repair shops.

2. Find the company on LinkedIn, and send a connection request

3. Once the owner has accepted, mail out an informational package about how your referral program works.

4. Invite them to meet for coffee, lunch or dinner and get them signed up.

> **Your goal should be to have four of these meetings each week, from Tuesday thru Friday.**

CHAPTER 20

Contact These Businesses

Here's the businesses I'd start with...

Divorce attorneys.

Since one or more vehicles are usually involved in a divorce, attorneys who specialize in divorce can be a great source.

Even if you start out just by providing them with things like book values and market conditions that can help their clients get the full value for their vehicles, you'll establish your dealership as their trusted advisor. And this can make for a very profitable relationship.

Probate attorneys.

One of my super secret sources for referrals is probate attorneys.

Now, these professionals might not send you a lot of buying business, but you can purchase a lot of used cars from them.

When a vehicle's involved in probate, the family usually just wants to sell the car and divvy up the money.

> Make sure your used car manager connects with local probate attorneys, and you'll have a never-ending source of used vehicles.

Tow truck drivers.

This group also makes for great referral partners because they "know the business."

If a vehicle breaks down or gets damaged in a collision, the tow truck driver is one of the first people on the scene, and a lot people will trust his opinion.

Additionally, most tow truck drivers get paid by the hour, and a couple of referral fees each month could really help them out so make a point of getting to know the tow truck drivers in your area.

Small, independent repair shop owners.

This group might not be one you'd normally consider, but small, independent repair shops can make great referral partners.

They're in a unique position in the car business, because their clients often trust them implicitly.

And since every mechanic knows there are cases in which a vehicle isn't worth repairing, you should definitely not discount this group.

> **Independent repair shops will often also buy from your parts department, which can lead to an increase in your parts business.**

OB/GYN Doctors.

Okay, this next group will probably take you by surprise, but OB/GYN doctors are nonetheless a great source of referrals.

When a couple's expecting a new baby, they usually need to change their vehicle.

Because these doctors know about the new baby before any other businesses, it gives you a head start on bringing the couple into your marketing funnel.

The referral fee won't be that big of a deal to a doctor, so you should consider alternative rewards, such as...

- Donating a sum to her favorite charity

- Filling up her vehicle with gas

- Offering to detail all of her family's vehicles (they probably have somewhere between three and four cars)

- Providing some other service to her office staff

It's also worth considering some creative techniques that will help market the doctor's practice to patients, such as enabling the doctor to offer a new baby car seat and stroller for each vehicle that's bought at your dealership by a referral.

New parents are faced with so many costs, that the prospect of receiving between $500 and $800 worth of baby products is a huge attraction factor.

There are so many ways to capitalize on a relationship with an OB/GYN doctor, I'm sure you'll come up with something.

Pastors and churches.

They say to never discuss religion when selling, but in truth, pastors and churches can be a great source of referrals.

They know so many people in the community, plus, people trust them implicitly.

Again, pastors and other religious leaders aren't likely to be motivated by a referral fee, so you should offer to donate a sum to their organization for every referral.

This has the added benefit that it will likely get you a mention in their local church newsletter.

You know the old saying, "Birds of a feather flock together?"

It's true: People socialize at churches. It's not only about faith, it's also about community.

So talk to your staff and see how many local churches you can establish relationships with.

Loan officers.

Loan officers will send you a lot of car deals, but the process will be a bit longer than with other professionals.

Here's why: If a house is being sold or bought, it's usually an indication that a vehicle purchase is not far behind.

That means that mortgage brokers can provide a fairly accurate timeframe for when the prospect will be in the market for a car.

And of course, in addition to sending referrals, loan officers can actually help facilitate the financing process for you.

Reach out to some loan officers in your area, and build solid relationships with them.

Pediatric doctors and orthodontists.

If you have any vehicles priced between $5,000 and $15,000 on your lot, you need to get pediatric doctors and orthodontists as referral partners.

They often have great relationships with their patients and will see a steady stream of 16-year-old kids begging their parents for a vehicle.

What's more, they have every kid's birthday on file.

You could capitalize on that by offering to pay for birthday cards to be sent out with a coupon for reimbursement for driving school or $1,000 off a car from your dealership.

Office supply, copier repair and computer repair professionals.

This group is one that you probably see every day in your dealership, but you probably don't give them much thought.

You're going to want to target this this group for two reasons.

First, for their own driving needs, since they rack up a lot of miles every day.

Second, they spend their days in a variety of client businesses, which means they meet a lot of different people.

> **If you can get them excited about your referral program, it'll be like having your very own mobile sales staff.**

The number of referrals this group can generate for your dealership is staggering.

CPAs.

The best way to get to leaders in your community is through their CPAs.

Almost every business owner has to see his accountant at least once a year, so establishing a relationship with a CPA is a great way to cement your dealership as the trusted advisor.

Plus, if a business owner is referred to you by his CPA, chances are his employees will also hear about your dealership.

And that means that just a few connections can lead to a lot of car deals.

These are just a few of the types of businesses and professionals you can target.

Eventually, you should really contact every business owner or HR manager in your area and invite him to your referral program.

However, if you start with the list above, you'll be well on your way to expanding your referral program.

> **Imagine how many extra vehicles you can sell with only 1 referral partner from each business category sending you referrals!**

But I'm sure you're thinking where am I going to get a list of all these businesses?

Well I've solved that problem for you too…

Here's an application I've developed that will generate 1000's of business records on demand—in just seconds!

Check out InstantMarketingList.com where you'll be able to generate any local business list on demand.

CHAPTER 21

Build Your Audience

The next place to find people to get signed up for your referral program is through audiences.

Building an audience is all about connecting with people who share the same interests.

If you like to fly RC airplanes, you should be connecting with other enthusiasts and sponsoring related events.

If you like to run, get involved with the running community.

Take an hour or two and brainstorm with your staff.

Each staff member has at least one hobby or passion.

> **Ask you employees to help get people signed up through their social circles.**

The best part about building an audience this way is that you can do it both in your local community and outside of your market.

Because you share a similar interest with these people, you'll have the opportunity to meet a lot of potential clients and establish solid relationships with them.

As a result, you'll get deeply entrenched in the community.

> **You can also build your audience by offering your expertise to other professionals in your area.**

For example, if a local attorney is sponsoring a seminar on how to file bankruptcy, you should contact her and offer to speak about how to buy a vehicle after filing.

Cover topics such as what documentation auto lenders will want to see and how debt-to-income ratios work.

In short, offer her the opportunity to share insider insights about the car business with her clients.

Now, when that attorney is in the market for a new car, who do you think she'll go to first?

And who do you think she'll refer her friends to?

There's always some professional or organization offering a seminar or workshop in your area, which means that there are many more opportunities to share your expertise.

Here's a few places to start with...

- Driving schools
- Car clubs
- Chamber of Commerce

- Community colleges

- Kiwanis

- Noon Lions

- Related Industries

- Public Speakers

- Life Events (Birth, Death, Divorce)

- Financial Planners

Keep thinking; the audiences are endless.

CHAPTER 22

You're Not Making It Easy

The reason you're not getting very many referrals right now is because you're making it too difficult for your clients to send you a referral.

Some of you might argue with me, but let's break it down and put ourselves in your client's shoes for a minute.

Let's say a couple of months ago, you had a great experience at the dealership and wound up buying a car.

All the staff were super helpful and you received a fair price.

Now one of your co-workers is interested in buying a vehicle and asks you if you know of any good dealerships.

Since it's been a few months, you don't remember the name of the salesperson who helped you, so you decide to call the dealership and let them know you might have a referral for them.

But first you have to find the phone number…

Strike #1 – You're making the client take time to find your phone number.

In the three to five minutes it took for this client to find your phone number, he probably checked Facebook, received both a text message and an email and finally got distracted by his kids or work.

That means he's most likely forgotten all about sending you the referral.

Let's say the client does remember to call.

You call the dealership, and you get either an automated switchboard or the front desk operator.

You say, "Hi, My name is Gus Skarlis, and I have a friend who's interested in buying a car from your dealership."

Who is the operator trained to transfer the call to?

- A salesperson
- The Internet manager
- A sales manager
- The general sales manager
- The sales tower
- The client service department

Strike #2: You don't have a defined referral process in place.

What are the chances that this possible referral doesn't reach the right person?

Pretty likely.

What happens if the call does get transferred to the correct persons and that staff member is busy with another client, away for the day or unable to answer his phone?

Hopefully, the operator will pick up and take a message.

But what if that doesn't happen, or if the call goes to voice mail?

> **That means you have a high probability of losing this referral... not to mention upsetting the client who was trying to help you.**

Are you beginning to see how many things can go wrong during the initial stage of just trying to contact your dealership to give them a referral?

It's too difficult for your clients to connect and contact you — and that's a reason why you're not receiving referrals.

Here's another example that you'll be able to relate too...

Let's say you've just joined a fitness center.

You're absolutely in love with it.

You talk about it at work, with your friends over dinner, you even mention it to your buddies on the golf course.

Now let's take it a little further:

One of your friends asks you, "Hey, I'm thinking about joining that new fitness center. Who should I talk to over there?"

> **You give them the name of the person who assisted you when you signed up to become a member... but that's the end of the conversation.**

Pretty normal how this happened, right?

I mean, it's a perfect example of a possible referral to the new fitness center.

But did you notice what just happened?

You gave your friend your contact's name, and that's helpful.

But that was end of the conversation.

You didn't give him any way to contact the fitness center.

And you didn't let the fitness center know you were the person who gave the referral.

Now your friend, who only has the name of your contact at the fitness center, will have to go on the Internet, look up the fitness center's phone number and possibly get directions.

With all of the distractions in life, what are the chances that your friend will actually ask for that person when he visits the fitness center?

Probably not very likely. Is this sounding strangely familiar?

CHAPTER 23

Solutions

After all the years I've spent in the car business, I know the above scenarios are consistent with every car dealer and just about every business for that fact, so don't feel bad if this happens at your store.

Here's the solution so the above scenarios will turn those missed referral conversations into referral prospects.

When I started selling cars back in 1994 I started my own referral program and used a page from my Uncle George's playbook.

Here's how it worked...

Back in the 1970s in Waterloo, Iowa, my Uncle George started a home improvement business.

His entire marketing plan consisted of going out every day and knocking on doors, cold calling and sending out direct mail letters.

Uncle George's business became wildly successful thanks to his referral strategy.

You see, what Uncle George did was this: Every time he landed a job, he would leave 10 or 20 postcards for the client.

The front of the postcard looked like a $100 bill.

On the back, there were lines for the name, address and phone number of the prospect.

Below that was a line for the contact details of the person who referred him.

Uncle George did this because he knew the neighbors would come over and look at the new windows, siding and gutters.

And when they did they always had questions about how much it would cost to update their house too.

Because every house and job is different Uncle George wanted to make it easy for his new clients so...

All they had to do was to fill out the postcard, mail it in and my Uncle George would call them and give the a **FREE** estimate.

But the genius part was that these postcards were stamped postage pre-paid.

And since there wasn't any postage necessary, all a client had to do was fill out the information and drop it any mailbox.

Can you get any simpler than that?

Now, every time uncle George sold a deal from a referral, he'd personally go to the referrer's home to thank him and give him a crisp $100 bill.

It was a brilliant win-win that created a multi-million dollar business based on these simple postcards - **and it's because they were easy for his clients to use.**

My uncle George still uses them today, almost 40 years later, and still with great results.

Because I had so much development experience and knew that technology is the gateway to human interaction.

All did was take uncle George's postcard idea, which was simple, easy and non-interrupting, and instead of postcards, I substituted text messaging.

It met all the criteria that the postcard did: simple, quick and easy to use.

The platform I developed for generating more referrals **uses text messaging as the communication channel.**

Instead of making your clients find your phone number, call and hope someone get's the correct lead information...

> **Once your clients sign up they'll receive a text message with instructions to save the phone number in their contacts as "Your Dealerships Referral Hotline"**

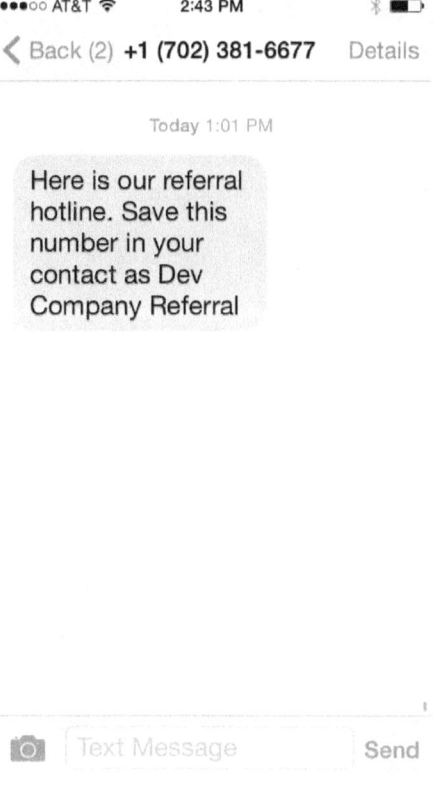

Then when they have a referral they can quickly text you the referral prospects information and start a conversation via text message.

The best part about a text messaging system is that pretty much everyone has a cell phone and knows how to text message.

That means you won't have to teach or show your clients how to send you referrals.

In fact, most of your clients will actually appreciate the fact that you're making it easy for them.

It's simple.

Plus, all your of these leads are stored in an admin area so you'll never lose or misplace a referral again.

CHAPTER 24

Getting More Referrals Has Nothing To Do With Your Reputation

Most dealers think that they can tout all the reasons why a person should buy a vehicle from their dealership and they'll receive referrals but in reality none of it matters.

What really matters is this…

Before your clients are going to send you a referral they need to know **for a fact** their family and friends are going to be treated fair and taken care of.

That's all they care about…

> **Until you can prove to your clients that you CAN and WILL do that you're not going to receive referrals.**

Getting more referrals is all about your clients reputation… NOT YOURS!

Let's go back in time to when the referral opportunity got started.

Your dealership's client Mary has a conversation with her co-worker Gwen about buying a vehicle.

Mary tells Gwen that your dealership was great, everyone was nice and she should consider your dealership.

A few days later Gwen shows up at your dealership looking to buy a vehicle.

It's a disaster, Gwen has credit issues, she owes more on her vehicle than it's worth and she spends 6 hours finding out that she can't buy a vehicle unless she has $7000 cash down.

Gwen goes back and tells Mary off.

"Why did you send me to those guys, they were terrible. I'll never go to them again."

Mary, not knowing the entire story is now upset with your dealership too.

Gwen and Mary's relationship has even lost a little bit trust.

This is why your clients do not send you referrals.

They **do not and will not** put their reputation on the line.

It all could have been avoided if your dealership just had a referral content strategy in place.

CHAPTER 25

New Client Kit

I call the content strategy our New Client Kit and it's very simple to develop because all you have to do is...

> **Answer the questions going on in your prospect's head.**

Before anyone buys anything, they need to have their questions answered.

The old saying is that there are no objections just unanswered questions.

Here's a great exercise to get you started...

If your mom were going to buy a car and you couldn't accompany her to the dealership, what questions would you want to make sure she asked before buying?

Write down those questions.

Then answer them clearly and comprehensively.

Next, put this information together in the form of reports, charts, graphs, infographics and videos.

This will be the start of your Dealerships New Client Kit.

> **By providing this information, you're showing your dealership is transparent about the buying process.**

And willing to answer any questions the prospect may have.

It solves 2 problems…

Mary now knows that you will be sending her family and friends relevant information about the vehicle buying process at your dealership.

…And you'll be immediately starting your sales process with Gwen.

Simultaneously, you're creating an opportunity to edu-sell and present the exact content and information you want them to see.

And guess what happens?

> **Your dealership will instantly build trust and credibility.**

CHAPTER 26

Answer These Questions

Here are some content ideas to get you started building your New Client Kit.

Should you buy or lease?

Create a few scenarios depicting who should buy and who should lease. Explain that if you drive over 20,0000 miles per year, you shouldn't lease.

However, if you're only going to keep the vehicle for a few years, then you might want to consider a lease.

Cover some of the myths about leasing, and explain your manufacturer's guidelines, including those pertaining to early buyouts, as well as wear and tear.

Do I really need an extended warranty?

This is a great opportunity to introduce extended warranties.

Discuss the difference between exclusionary and named-component coverage, deductibles, transfers, cancellations and financing options (BUDCO).

Also talk about your current labor rates and components that often fail in your geographic area.

What is GAP insurance?

Create a chart about GAP insurance and what it covers.

When I was in finance, I would advise my clients to raise their deductible to $1000, since this savings would cover the cost of the GAP Insurance.

How does my credit score affect my interest rate?

Here you can talk about how lenders can use three different bureaus, and how some lenders will allow you to use the highest score while others use a specific bureau.

Explain that there are also different scores, such as Auto score, and that lenders look at length of employment, income, previous payment history and other relevant factors when they make a decision.

Highlight the advantages of allowing the dealership to arrange financing because a dealer works with anywhere from 4 to 30 different lenders to help secure the best overall program for each client.

What is a certified pre-owned vehicle?

Create a report that explains a bit more about your certified pre-owned program, warranties, financing rates and certified requirements.

Make sure that it's clear why they're such a good value.

Should-ask questions and pointers

This is a list of questions that only someone in the car business would know to ask.

When you include these, you're helping your prospect by making him aware of some of the things he otherwise wouldn't know.

At the same time, it can help him realize other dealerships might be lying to him.

Questions can include...

Have the dealer call to get a 10-day payoff.

The reason is that some dealers make estimates based on the credit bureaus' scores, and they could be financing a higher amount than necessary.

Providing this information will help you get a lower balance to finance, and that means lower payments.

If you're trading in a vehicle, ask the dealer to call the warranty company and see if they have any refunds or cancellations coming from products such as extended warranties, gap insurance or maintenance plans.

The reason is that if you did have previous products, you're very likely to want them again.

Plus, it will give you a lower balance to finance and improve your LTV for a better call.

If you're leasing, check to see if there's a disposition or termination fee.

You need to know this upfront, before signing.

This way, there are no surprises in the event you come back in a few years to term or buy out the vehicle.

Ask if there is any pre-payment penalty on the finance contract.

Most lenders don't have a pre-payment penalty, but it's always good to remember to ask the question.

Ask to see the credit reports the dealer pulled.

You should see the score and the actual report, and make copies for your own records. This will benefit you.

Dealers want you to see your score and your reports, because if you need to see different lender programs, you'll know the dealer was being upfront from the get go.

Especially if you're a subprime client, the dealer might have a lender with a higher rate but less money down, and you'll be able to see the information the lender is basing its decision on.

If the dealer offers e-contracting in the finance department, ask the finance manager to print out copies of the contract before you sign them.

This will give you additional peace of mind with e-contracting.

Ask which lender the contract is being sent to and get their mailing address and phone number so you have a point of contact.

By doing this, if you have a question about the contract or payments, you can call the lender directly instead of trying to track down the dealership's finance managers.

If you're buying a pre-owned vehicle, ask to see the car fax and the dealership's repair order.

This allows you to see exactly what work has been done on the vehicle and when.

The dealership should show you the car fax no matter what; but by reviewing the repair order, you can also see the expenses of reconditioning the vehicle.

This eliminates come backs, as any mechanical or cosmetic issues can be clarified before you leave the dealership.

By offering all of this information before a prospect even asks for it, you're positioning your dealership as an authority and a leader.

And that's what will make a prospect want to buy from you.

> **Getting the client engaged is the first step to the sale and content is the best way to do that.**

Once you receive a referral you should immediately mail out your New Client Kit to your new prospect.

CHAPTER 27

Build Value

Building additional value and reasons to buy from your dealership is not a new concept and every dealer uses the "why buy here" marketing strategy but here's how to take it to the next level and leave your competition in the dust.

You and every other dealer probably offer free car washes, tires for life or some other promotion.

Set your dealership apart by offering unique benefits, such as a large number of master technicians, free loaners, free shuttle, free carwashes, free client lounge and free Wi-Fi.

If clients can do business in more than one language at your place, then that's an asset, too.

Make a list of all of the benefits and include it in your New Client Kit.

For example:

When you buy a vehicle from ABC Motors, you'll receive all of these benefits at no charge:

- *Unlimited FREE car washes ($300 value): When your vehicle needs a quick rinse and shine, bring it by and use our state of the art brushless car wash! Don't use the outdated car washes around town that will only scratch up your vehicle. When you buy from us, you can use our car wash as many times as you want at no additional cost to you!*

- *FREE Shuttle: ($200 value): When you need to be somewhere but your vehicle's being serviced, don't worry: use our free shuttle to get you to your appointment! Unlike other dealerships where you have to wait around for hours while your car's being fixed or pay for a loaner vehicle, we offer free shuttle rides for our clients!*

Now, of course you want to point all of this out to your prospects.

However, you need to think like an entrepreneur and take building value a step further.

When it comes to building value and offering services to set your company apart from the rest, Google probably does it best.

When you sign up for a Gmail account, you don't just get free email.

You also get free cloud storage, free documents, free spreadsheets, free presentations, free file sharing, free chat, a free calendar and more.

Sure, you can go on the Internet and find all of these services for free with other companies.

What you won't find is the ability to use and manage all of them from one single location.

And that's where Google has set itself apart by creating a virtual ecosystem where users can do pretty much anything pertaining to communication with a single account.

Now, how can you apply this insight to your dealership?

The answer is simple: to build value, you have to think beyond free car washes and oil changes.

CHAPTER 28

Make It Impossible For Your Competitors

Here's you are going to make it impossible for your competitors to compete with you.

> **This is a very advanced referral marketing strategy and should only be implemented AFTER you have done the previous steps.**

You know those cards that kids in your community used to sell?

They each had $100 worth of coupons, but the cards themselves only cost $10.

You've seen similar coupon books and cards everywhere—and for a good reason: People use them!

We all know the biggest expense for a local business is advertising.

Every business is always looking for more clients and leads.

I'm sure you've received those mailers with a bunch of coupons like Valpak and so on.

Local businesses all put in some coupons or discounts and send it out consumers in their neighborhood.

To build value for your dealership, all you have to do is take that same idea and negotiate with local companies to give you coupons for free or heavily discounted services.

Then you put them in your New Client Kit and give them to your clients when they buy.

So not only are you offering the reasons why they should buy from you but now you are giving them coupons and discounts on products and services that they are going to be using.

> **My favorite businesses to approach first are restaurants, because most of them are happy to give you a free $5 or $10 gift card.**

The restaurant knows that once the client enters, he'll spend more money than the value of the gift card.

And this client might not have come to this restaurant without the gift card as an incentive.

In short, it's a great lead generation strategy for them.

If you've ever done any pay-per-click or Facebook advertising, you know that participating businesses are paying $5 or more for each click.

Now, what you're offering is to bring local companies buyers and leads.

It doesn't cost them anything unless the lead comes in— yet they receive free branding, advertising and market awareness.

Contact every restaurant in your area.

You'll be surprised... most will thank you for helping them out.

What's more: most restaurants have 10 or more employees that you've just established a relationship with.

And that means they're all potential clients.

My advice is to contact a wide array of family-owned restaurants, so you'll have gift cards for pizza, Chinese, subs, steaks, seafood, Italian, sports bars, Thai, deli's, bakeries and so on.

You can even parter with businesses located outside of your market, because people are often curious about new places, and with a new vehicle, they won't mind the drive.

Plus, it gives you the opportunity to network and build even more relationships which effectively expands your reach.

Other types of businesses that are great potential partners are pet stores, kids' activities, coffee shops, chiropractors, insurance agents, storage units, travel agencies, miniature golf courses, game arcades and movie theaters.

Remember: Anything related to entertainment is always a good choice, since people enjoy recreational activities.

Spend some time networking with as many local companies as possible but...

> **Remember, the relationship is about depth not width.**

If you get between 20 and 200 participating businesses, with coupons and discounts your competition won't stand a chance, because now buying a vehicle from your dealership has far more value than just a free car wash or a couple of oil changes.

In addition, if just one employee from every partner business buys a vehicle from you, your dealership will see substantial growth

...All simply from helping out local companies.

The first dealer to set this up in their area WINS. So get started right now.

CHAPTER 29

How Much To Pay For A Referral?

Right now, you're probably paying a $100 to $200 fee for every referral that converts into a sale.

However, most dealers average between $300 and $800 in advertising spend for each vehicle they sell.

> **This means you're willing to give the TV networks, radio stations and newspapers tens of thousands of dollars each month – without any guarantee of a sale.**

What's more, if you're still signed up with them - you're giving TrueCar $300 for each deal.

Your TrueCar sales are all invoice buyers who probably aren't going to finance with you, nor buy any aftermarket products, come to you for servicing or send you any referrals.

Let's put this in even more perspective.

If you go out for a nice dinner and have a few drinks, it's difficult to keep the tab under $100.

With these comparisons in mind, you need to adjust your thinking. You need to look at paying out a referral fee that makes sense for your clients' time and effort.

Regardless of what payout you give as a referral fee, you're still missing the most important number.

CHAPTER 30

Lifetime Client Value

In my meetings with venture capitalists, I found out that they all looked at one number when doing their business valuations:

<u>*Lifetime Client Value*</u>

> Venture capitalists don't care it if costs $100 in marketing spend to acquire a client for a $10 per month product – if the client stays on board for 41 months and makes that same $10 or more purchase each month.

Because 41 months x $10 = $410 - $100 acquisition costs = $310 gross profits.

And this is where you're missing the real revenue stream.

The real value of your dealership is in client lifetime value.

If you estimate a $1,500 profit for each car sale you make, and a client will buy four vehicles from you during his lifetime, then that client isn't worth just $1,500; he's worth $6,000!

And that's even without figuring in parts, servicing or aftermarket profits.

> **This is why you need to think like an entrepreneur and look at the lifetime value of a client, not just a one-time transaction.**

I know dealers who are paying out between $600 and $2,000 for each referral because they realize that amount is a drop in the bucket compared the long-term value that the dealership will receive from these additional clients.

"Lifetime Client Value is the most important metric you should be looking at."

Go pull your statement and look at your profits and adjust your referral fee accordingly because no matter what you pay for a referral fee - you don't pay the fee unless you sell the vehicle.

CHAPTER 31

How To Pay Your Referral Fees

Getting checks cut for your referrers is probably the most frustrating part of running a referral program but fortunately there's a solution that makes it easier for you to pay out your referral fees.

We all know it takes time to get your referrers paid.

Unfortunately, this is where most dealerships drop the ball.

Let's say you get a referral from a client, and you sell a vehicle to that referral.

Now, what are the steps to get the check cut at your dealership?

Hopefully you wait until the deal is financed.

Then, you have to:

- Make sure the referral fee was set up in the deal by the sales manager so your costs are correct.
- Fill out a check request form.
- Get the check request signed by a manager or the general manager.

- Take the check request to the business office and give it to the appropriate person.
- Wait for the business office to cut the check.
- Wait for the general manager or owner to sign the check.
- Call the client to ask them to pick the check up or, if they can't come to the dealership, mail it to them.

If this sounds like a lot of steps, the truth is, it *is*.

But the really frustrating thing is what's happening every few days during this process:

The referrer is calling or emailing you asking about his referral check.

Getting your referrer paid is a process.

Remember, when it's difficult for your clients to send you referrals they won't.

Well, if you make it hard for them to get paid, they won't send you referrals, either. It's not worth their time.

Well, here's an interesting tidbit of information.

VISA now offers an arrangement that makes paying out your referral fees super simple.

> **Once a client signs up for your referral program, he's issued a VISA card with your dealerships information on it.**

Then when he sends you a referral and that referral buys a vehicle...

- You can select any amount to pay the referrer.

- You can Electronically add funds to their card and they can spend it anywhere VISA is accepted.

Just imagine how much hassle this will eliminate for you!

But the real benefit is that with the reloadable card you can now think outside the box and expand your program into lead generation.

Let me give you an example…

Since you've got a few insurance agents signed up for your referral program you can pay them $10 per lead they send you instead of a flat fee if the prospect buys.

Or if it's the end of the month and you need to sell a few more vehicles to hit a stair step bonus you could text message your referral sign ups and increase your referral payouts on specific vehicles.

You can even set up fast start or fast finish contests all because you can quickly message your database and have the flexibility to pay them any amount you'd like.

Plus, by providing your clients with the VISA card, your dealership gains top of mind awareness, because they'll always carry that card with your information on it with them.

The only drawback is that it costs approximately $15,000 to set up this arrangement.

We've developed a partnership with VISA where ReferralDriven.com can set your dealership up with their own VISA branded card for a small per card activation and load fee.

This will save you the $15,000 VISA set up fee and give you a great way to build your brand and pay your referrers instantly.

If you have any questions regarding the VISA card program please email me at gus@referraldriven.com

CHAPTER 32

Hire A Referral Manager

If you really, really want more referrals hire a referral manager.

This can start out as an entry-level position that pays between $2,000 and $3,000 per month— but the upside is, the potential returns are virtually unlimited.

Even if you're located in a small town, you can start to network in larger markets.

If you're in a large market, you can funnel even more business to your dealership.

> **You should be treating your referral department just like your sales, parts, finance and service departments.**

Because even if you haven't ever thought of it this way, it's a separate profit center.

Referrals are a marketing channel just like TV, radio, social media and direct mail.

The only difference is that you can use all mediums to connect with referrers.

Get a dedicated referral manager, because they can help grow your referral program at a much faster pace.

Again, this can be an entry-level position.

I would hire someone who's outgoing, knows a bit about social media and knows how to network.

You want someone who's very social and is willing to talk to anyone.

Someone who enjoys going to meetings and events.

> **A good referral manager will have between eight and ten meeting each week; will make a few hundred phone calls per week; and be active on social media, including LinkedIn.**

This position is not a selling position, but rather a networking position.

A good hire could be a former chamber of commerce employee, event planner, visitor center representative or even a local celebrity.

The job goal will be to get as many people signed up for your referral program as possible; to network with local businesses; and to promote your referral program.

Additionally, it includes create strategic alliances and finding ways your dealership can help add value to the community.

We've written a manual that will train the person you select to become your referral manager.

Get in contact with us to purchase copies.

Once you have a referral department set up, you can start generating referrals for just about any department at your dealership.

CHAPTER 33

You're Not Thinking Big Enough

People don't just want to buy cars, they need to take care of their vehicles, too.

That means you can ask for referrals for every aspect of your business that sells a product or service—and if you don't, you're missing out on sales opportunities.

So create a referral plan that includes your F&I department, parts department and body shop because they all can and should be receiving referrals too.

> **How many people buy a vehicle from a private party on Craig's List and then go to WarrantyDirect.com to buy a warranty.**

With a referral program in place when that conversation happens you'll at least have a chance to possibly get that extended warranty referral because your clients know they can earn money if they send that prospect to you.

CHAPTER 34

21 Advanced Referral Strategies

Now we are going to talk about some advanced marketing strategies that you can implement with your referral program.

Take Warby Parker, the eyeglass company, as an example.

They allow you to pick up to five free samples of their eyeglasses to try on at home.

They even pay for shipping both ways.

The client doesn't pay a dime until he decides to buy a pair.

There are many examples of successful referral program stratgies out there you just need to start looking for them.

To get you started here's a list of the top 21 referral strategies that you can implement in your dealership right now.

1. Overnight Test Drives: For example, you could offer from home test drives or overnight test drives to referral clients.

For a prospect who gets home late from work, it's a great opportunity.

He doesn't have to drive all the way to your dealership, plus, he can do the test drive after work, which means his weekend is still free.

If you don't want to offer overnight test drives for insurance reasons, you could offer a coupon for a rental car of the same make and model at Enterprise or Avis.

It'll cost you about $30 on a rental vehicle to create a great client experience and a great opportunity to sell a car.

The client gets to drive the vehicle on the roads he uses, park it in his own garage, show it to his neighbors and get a real feel for whether the vehicle will work for him or not.

Plus, just the mental ownership of that vehicle will bring him one step closer to buying.

2. Bonus Levels: You could offer referrers a free vacation or tickets to Disney World after sending 10 referrals.

3. Millennials. I'm 40 right now, and when my parents have a question about computers, cell phones or the Internet, guess who they call?

Me!

Everyone's talking about marketing to Millennials, and I agree; you absolutely need to market to them.

But what everyone's forgetting is that all of these Millennials are influencing their parents' buying decisions.

So the potential of this group isn't just about referrals: it's also about providing them with great information about the value added benefits of your dealership so they'll advise their parents to buy from you.

Hire a few young salespeople and get them involved in groups and activities.

4. Provide holiday cards for your top 100 clients.

Find out which clients spent the most at your dealership, and for the top 100, offer to pay for their Holiday cards.

Hire a local photographer and send your clients to their location for the shoot and then pay for all printing, mailing and photography costs.

Ask them to send you their lists of family and friends so you can send each of these people a card.

Then a few weeks later send each person on the list an invitation to join your referral program. Genius Right!

5. Establish business plan pricing by taking a play out of the Ford playbook.

Set up business plan pricing for every company you contact. Just like Ford has A, Z, X, D plan pricing you should have pricing programs for every business in your area too.

Set up a plan that offers employees of these businesses some special promotion, for example additional discounts, VIP treatment or some other incentive.

This strategy makes the businesses feel special, and you'll get more sales from the employees.

Plus, they'll be excited to refer their friends to you.

You can even approach businesses as far as 120 miles outside of your area, because people don't mind driving for a great experience.

6. Publish a monthly hard copy newsletter.

This is probably the number one marketing thing you can do to grow your referral program - send out a monthly hard copy newsletter.

I used to publish one when I was working in my dad's dealership. It was called Junior's Journal (I'm a Jr.), and it worked great!

I'd include questionnaires for readers to fill out and send back to me along with a picture and their contact information, and then I'd select a "business of the month" that I'd feature in the next newsletter.

I'd also include birthday wishes; a calendar of the local events in town; information about new vehicles; and a few other articles.

It was only six pages in total, but people loved getting it each and every month.

7. Host events and fundraisers.

You have a big parking lot and a huge indoor space, so start using it to host local events and fundraisers.

Call your local Chamber of Commerce, churches, kids' groups and schools, and offer to host any events they're planning.

By showing goodwill, people will feel obligated to send you clients, and they'll also be more interested in buying from you.

Plus, it gives your dealership more exposure and people will be more familiar with it.

8. Set up Google alerts and use social media.

Social media is a great way to interact with your referral partners and get noticed by their followers.

It's also one of the most valuable marketing tools your dealership has.

But if people aren't following you, they're not hearing about your dealership.

In order to interact, you need to have something relevant to talk about—and this is a big challenge for many dealerships.

Every time a new referral partner signs up, set up a Google alert about his industry.

Then when some interesting information comes along, create a Facebook or Twitter post about it and tag the referral partner.

> **This kills three birds with one stone: You're being social, you're also tagging a partner so he has more content for his feed and you're reaching his followers as well as your own.**

You can also find out what people are talking about or want to know about on social media, and generate valuable content about those topics.

9. Monitor conversations by setting up alerts for your dealership and brand names.

For example, you'd set up alerts for "Gus Skarlis Honda," "Jeep," "new and used," "financing" and "pre-approval."

Though you can set up a general keyword alert in Google, it doesn't narrow the results down to just social media, which means you'll be getting news, articles, blogs and advertising results.

To really make sure you're only getting results from social media mentions, use search tools that are specifically designed for this purpose.

Tweetdeck, Hootsuite and Twilert are great apps for Twitter; Backtype works well for Facebook; and INK361 is specifically designed to search on Instagram.

> We've integrated some great tools into the ReferralDriven.com platform that will automate most of this data capture for you.

10. Start giving referrals.

If you want more referrals, you need to start giving them out.

If you have a client and you can't get financing for him, send him over to a BHPH dealer.

Don't worry, they'll send you referrals too, because they'll know people who want to buy new vehicles. Plus, they'll probably pay you a referral fee as well.

In addition, you should review your client list to determine how many of your clients have their own businesses.

Then start referring them to related service professionals such as detail shops, glass repair businesses, tire stores, etc.

11. Advertise these businesses in your monthly newsletter and on your website.

You know how hotels have a rack of brochures for local events and attractions at the reception or the concierge's desk?

12. Buy a display rack, and when a business signs up for your referral program, give it a place on your rack for its business cards and brochures.

13. Organize a "Ride and Drive."

I'm not sure if this is still done, but when I was selling cars, every time a new model or redesigned vehicle was introduced to the market, the dealers would rent a track or parking lot, get a few of the competitors' vehicles and let the sales team drive the heck out of them.

You should be doing the same thing.

In fact, you should make it a yearly event at your dealership.

> **The only requirements is that every visitor must bring a friend.**

This way, you get to introduce your current client to the new vehicle, as well as meet someone who is not yet a client and get on his or her radar.

14. Set up a REAL Business Development Center.

If you have in-house telemarketing that targets your existing clients, your problem is that you're only trying to generate more sales from clients who have already bought from you.

Your goal should be to connect with your clients, get them signed up for your referral program and sell to their friends and family.

You'll grow your business by 300% if you focus on connections, not sales.

There are data mining tools and applications that will alert you when your clients have equity and lease maturity.

Focus your tele-marketing department on getting as many of your clients to sign up for your referral program as possible.

15. Hold a credit repair seminar.

A lot of people have bad credit, so you could joint venture with a local loan officer and credit restoration specialist to hold a credit seminar about how to buy a vehicle and vehicle with bad credit.

These types of seminars are very easy to set up, and they can bring you a captive audience of people who will trust your dealership.

16. Partner with driving schools.

Connect with the driving schools in your area and offer to sponsor them.

There are many ways you can market to this group and provide value to them, such as offering a $1,000 discount on a vehicle for every graduate.

17. Join and comment on blogs.

Join all of the relevant blogs for the car makes you sell. When you get a new one of these vehicles in, you can do an email blast to their reader list.

18. Find car enthusiasts.

Get a list of car enthusiasts in your area, and invite them to events at your dealership.

You can organize mixers, talks by manufacturers' representatives or even presentations by fellow enthusiasts.

The point is to provide fun events where this group can come together to talk about cars and car clubs.

You could even sponsor their blog or invite them to guest blog for you.

19. Expect referrals.

You shouldn't just ask for referrals; you should actually make it a condition of doing business with you.

Before you go out and shake hands on a car deal, tell the client,

"I'm going to accept your offer and take a very small deal, but only if you agree to this one condition: You must send me one referral in the next 12 months. Now, when you get back to the finance department, my finance manager will go over the details with you. Sound fair?"

The prospect will always say yes, because it's never a problem to send a referral to you.

And when he finds out he'll get a fee for every referral that converts to a sale, he'll be even more excited to send his friends to you.

20. Send out calendars.

Print and send out yearly calendars to all your clients and referral partners.

Whether they hang it in their office, kitchen or games room, they'll have a 24/7 visual reminder of your dealership.

21. Connect with business opportunity seekers.

Business opportunity seekers are people who want to make more money, so they're looking for a second income or part-time work.

You should absolutely get these people signed up for your referral program because it's their objective to make money and they'll actively promote your business.

CHAPTER 35

Action Steps

Hopefully, you're excited right now about the idea of getting your referral program "restarted" and I've given you some great information to get started.

Moving forward here's the steps you need to take:

- Get as many people signed up as possible.

- Make it easy to communicate with you via text message.

- Put a content strategy in place with a New Client Kit.

- Make it easy to pay your referral fees.

There are many more strategies and ides that can help grow your dealership and I share them on my Podcast, Twitter, Periscope, Meerkat and LinkedIn.

So let's talk about how we can help "Restart" your referral program.

For more information and to connect with me please visit:

ReferralDriven.com